Patty's Pictures

by Leah Janovich
illustrated by Paige Billin-Frye

SCHOLASTIC INC.

New York • Toronto • London • Auckland
Sydney • Mexico City • New Delhi • Hong Kong

ISBN 978-0-545-24820-4

Copyright © 2010 by Lefty's Editorial Services.

All rights reserved. Published by Scholastic Inc.

SCHOLASTIC, READ & UNDERSTAND, and associated logos
are trademarks and/or registered trademarks of Scholastic Inc.

12 11 10 9 8 7 6 5 4 3 2 1   11 12 13 14 15 16/0

Printed in the U.S.A.   40
First printing, February 2011

Note to Parents & Teachers

Many children can read every word of a story, yet still struggle to understand its meaning. That's where the Read & Understand series comes in! These lively books contain two types of quick comprehension boosters:

1. **PAGE PROMPTS**—for children to verbally respond to after a page is read

2. **STORY PROMPTS**—for children to verbally respond to after the whole story is read

How do these prompts promote comprehension? When children answer engaging questions about text, their brains are activated to predict, visualize, infer, connect, and more deeply understand a story's meaning. Research shows that teaching kids to "think aloud" about stories helps them develop instant comprehension strategies that they can apply to everything they read.

This special series is also designed to build reading confidence. Toward that end, the stories feature predictable text, highly supportive pictures, and kid-pleasing plots.

Share these super-fun books with children today and they'll read with greater ease and comprehension for years to come!

Yippee! Patty and her family were going on vacation. Patty packed her brand-new camera. She planned to take lots and lots of pictures.

 Peek in Patty's backpack. What else is she bringing on the trip?

On the first day of vacation, Patty visited a lighthouse. It was right by the ocean.

"This will make the perfect picture!" she said.

Patty pointed her camera at the scene. *SNAP*.

QUESTION

Why do you think Patty wants to take pictures on her vacation?

But when Patty looked at the picture, she was disappointed. It was blurry.

"Oh well," she said, "I will just have to take the perfect picture tomorrow."

The next day, Patty visited a tall mountain. It was covered with snow.

"This will make the perfect picture!" she said.

Patty pointed her camera at the scene. *SNAP.*

What is the name of the mountain?

But when Patty looked at the picture, she was disappointed. The top of the mountain was missing.

"Oh well," she said, "I will just have to take the perfect picture tomorrow."

The next day, Patty visited a waterfall. It was late and the sun was setting.

"This will make the perfect picture!" she said.

Patty pointed her camera at the scene. *SNAP.*

But when Patty looked at the picture, she was disappointed. It was way too dark. You could barely see the waterfall.

Patty was very frustrated.

"Oh well," she said, "I will just have to take the perfect picture tomorrow."

Why do you think Patty feels frustrated?

On the last day of vacation, Patty visited a forest. What a perfect spot for a family portrait! Patty set the camera's timer. Then she put the camera on a rock and raced to join her mom, dad, and brother.

"Everyone say cheese," said Patty.

"Cheeeeeeeeeeeeeese!" said everyone.

But nothing happened.

 Do you like having your picture taken? Why or why not?

11

Tick, tick, tick...several seconds passed. It was hard to stand still and everyone started moving. *SNAP*. The camera finally took the photo.

"Ugh!" said Patty, "I'm afraid to even look at this one."

But when she did, she was surprised. Something amazing had happened!

PREDICT **What do you think might have happened?**

A deer and a baby fawn had wandered into the scene.

"Wow!" said Patty's mom.

"Incredible!" said her dad.

"Awesome!" said her brother.

"I finally took the perfect picture," said Patty. "It will help me remember this family vacation forever!"

TIE UP

How do you think Patty feels now?

Story Prompts

Answer these questions after you have read the book.

1 Can you retell this story in your own words?

2 Do you have a favorite photo of yourself or your family? Describe it.

3 When she gets home, Patty decides to take a photo of her pet gerbil. What happens? Turn on your imagination and tell a story about it.